Y0-AJO-559

**Like the book?
You'll love the online course!!**

http://bit.ly/FSCFMConfAttendee
To receive 15% off TODAY.

FUNDRAISING SUCCE$$:

BOARD ENGAGEMENT & EMPOWERMENT IN THE FUNDRAISING PROCESS

Liz Wooten Reschke, MPA, CGT

Louanne Saraga Walters

Copyright © 2016 Connectivity Community Consulting, My Video Voice Productions LLC

All rights reserved. In accordance with the U.S. Copyright Act of 1976, the scanning, uploading, and electronic sharing of any part of this book without the permission of the publisher is unlawful piracy and theft of the authors' intellectual property.

Please purchase only authorized editions, and do not participate in or encourage electronic piracy of copyrighted materials.

If you would like to use material from this book (other than for review purposes), prior written permission must be obtained by contacting the publishers at Louanne@MyVideoVoiceProductions.com or liz@connectformore.com.

Printed in the United States of America
FIRST EDITION

ISBN: 978-1533327468

TABLE OF CONTENTS

ACKNOWLEDGEMENT..3
INTRODUCTION..5
BOARD FUNDRAISING BASICS
    Fundraising Overview & It's Importance for
        the Nonprofit Sector................................10
    Basic Board Roles & Responsibilities...............15
    Why Do Board Members Need to Fundraise?.....21
    Building Relationships Takes Time (Or,
        Fundraising is a Process)..........................27
YOUR BOARD'S CURRENT INVOLVEMENT IN FUNDRAISING
    What's Your Board's Culture?........................32
    The Give or Get Policy..................................37
    Assessing Board's Comfort Level with
        Fundraising..41
    Assessing Your Board's Readiness to
        Fundraise..45
GETTING YOUR BOARD READY
    Motivation Strategies....................................50

  Board Member Education..............................54
  Working with Others in Development................58
  Role Play in the Board Room........................62
  Building Your Development Plan with
   the Board...65
WAYS BOARD MEMBERS CAN ASSIST IN FUNDRAISING
  Ways Your Board Can Participate in
   Fundraising..69
  Board's Role in the Ask................................73
  Board's Role in Donor Stewardship.................77
WAYS BOARD MEMBERS CAN LEAD FUNDRAISING
  Support & Selection of CEO/ED or Chief
   Development Officer................................82
  Fundraising Committee................................88
  Serving as a Donor/Sponsor.........................92
  Challenge and Matching Gifts.......................96
EVALUATION OF YOUR BOARD'S FUNDRAISING
  Sharing Successes at the Board Level............101
  Sharing Challenges at the Board/Committee
   Level..104
  Celebrating & Acknowledging Good Board
   Behavior..109
OTHER THOUGHTS
  Recruiting Fundraising Board Members...........114
  Duty of Loyalty & Conflicts of Interest.............118
SUMMARY AND RESOURCES
  Conclusion..123
  Appendix A..125
  Appendix B..142
  About the Authors......................................143

ACKNOWLEDGEMENT

I would like to thank the many folks in the nonprofit sector who continue to inspire and educate me in all things professional, personal and beyond. We are a caring bunch but it never hurts to combine thoughtful strategy with large hearts. Special thanks goes out to BoardSource, Carol Weisman and the countless other experts in our field. I am grateful to have such tremendous resources available to myself, my colleagues and my clients. Thank you for providing materials and insight so that we all may learn together as we serve.

I would also like to thank the nonprofit organizations who have both provided me the honor of serving on their board and working with their board through trainings and workshops. Board service is truly a labor of love, and I have been inspired and learned so much from all of you. Thank you for your dedicated and thoughtful service – keep up the good work and never stop learning!

I also want to express my immense gratitude to my family and friends for whom I gain strength and insight each and every day. I have been inspired by so many of them — educators, philanthropists, fighters, and tremendous human beings alike. I am honored to be surrounded by so many wonderful people and good examples of humanity. A special nod to my guardian angels who taught me the importance of philanthropy, community service, integrity and faith by their examples.

And finally, special thanks to my children. For the blessings and challenges of motherhood, for the intentionality of life and time well spent, and for filling my days with laughter and silliness. May you grow to realize your own potential and be uplifted just as I have... choosing to make a positive difference in this world in whichever way you navigate.

— Liz Wooten Reschke

INTRODUCTION

This book will help you understand the importance of a fundraising board in meeting your organization's mission, why and how board members can fundraise, how you can prepare your board to participate and lead fundraising activities, and how to evaluate and celebrate your board's fundraising efforts.

Seasoned board members and staffers charged with fundraising efforts alike will benefit from the comfortable discussion style as well as the many resources on empowering and engaging your board included in these pages.

Fundraising Succe$$: Board Engagement & Empowerment in the Fundraising Process is a summary of the online course containing over 3.0 hours of HD video.

Full participation in the online course, Fundraising Success: Board Engagement & Empowerment in the Fundraising Process, is approved for 3.5 points in Category 1.B – Education of the CFRE International application for initial certification and/or recertification.

About the Instructors:

Louanne Saraga Walters (LSW): Serving on a couple of nonprofit boards is what inspired me to leave my career as a financial advisor and move into the nonprofit sector. I felt empowered and completely engaged with my community, and I wanted to do even more! As a business owner, I'm now focused on helping nonprofits to reach greater capacity through online trainings and video production, and to learn new skills in marketing/communications, development, and self growth.

Liz Wooten Reschke (LWR): I have had the honor to serve many boards over the years... as staff, as facilitator/consultant and as board member/leader. Throughout my experience, engagement in fundraising has been one of the prominent challenges faced. A lot of what the challenges come down to, though, is engagement and empowerment of the entire board. That first starts with education for board members and staff working with them. As a consultant, I enjoy working collaboratively with leadership to help address board culture and empower effective board service, and provide resources to inspire engaged board work.

About this Book:

LWR: I've created this book to help the reader understand the roles and responsibilities of board members serving nonprofits. Some are ethical, some are legal, all are applicable to nonprofits of any size. So whether you're a nonprofit employee, current board member, or community volunteer considering serving on a board, I believe this book will be very helpful to you!

Through eight complete sections we'll learn how to:
- Increase fundraising results by engaging your board members
- Define board roles and responsibilities
- Create opportunities for board members to participate in fundraising at all levels
- Empower board members to lead fundraising efforts in their organizations
- Understand an effective partnership between board members, CEO's and professional fundraising staff
- Determine ways board members can participate in donor stewardship
- Create a committee structure that will enhance board fundraising efforts
- Provide board members with training to improve fundraising results
- Evaluate and celebrate board's fundraising efforts

- Recruit board members who will actively participate in development

LSW: Board members hold the same roles and responsibilities as outlined by BoardSource, regardless of size - but those actual duties that stem from the roles and responsibilities can be different with each nonprofit, correct?

LWR: Yes, each nonprofit board has its own unique characteristics and culture that define the specific tasks, say for example, how hands on your board is in the actual "Ask". But the overall roles and responsibilities are true regardless of nonprofit or size of nonprofit. I've written this curriculum in order to help guide a nonprofit in determining what their board tasks are according to their own board culture and readiness.

LSW: And to you, the reader: Where applicable, Liz has included additional resources and links for you to refer to and explore more in depth. We've also included them all in the back of the book, in Appendix A for easy access and reference.

So whenever you're ready, join us in the first section as Liz walks us through your board's roles and responsibilities.

BOARD FUNDRAISING BASICS

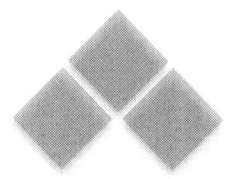

Chapter 1
Fundraising Overview & Its Importance for the Nonprofit Sector

LSW: In this first section, we're really covering the introductory basics - what is a nonprofit, what does a board do in serving a nonprofit, and why is a board important in the fundraising process?

LWR: Yes, from the beginning. The nonprofit sector started from people wanting to express their charity. If you think about it, it sprang from people who wanted to give back. The nonprofit, or 501(c)(3) is designed to 'serve the public good.'

Many people are not aware that there are 29 501(c) categories, and the 501(c)(3) or 501(c)(6) - such as a chamber of commerce or membership group - are the most popular or well known. But the term "nonprofit" is the whole range, from 1-29.

I like to say that nonprofits were formed as the selfish expression of people who wanted to make a change in their community, who wanted to give back. Because giving back makes us feel so good and so empowered!

LSW: I've heard that from many philanthropists and nonprofit employees who've felt they get more back from the giving than they felt they gave in the gift. To many, it's not an even exchange. The pleasure to give outweighs the gift!

Ok, we have the nonprofit - and that comes with tax exempt status, which means what?

LWR: Tax exempt status means it is a tax exempt entity, so the nonprofit may avoid sales tax in your state and for the IRS. And those who give donations to entities holding a tax exempt status have the ability to itemize those donations and lower their individual taxes. So the status is meant to encourage people to give monies and other items to help that entity create positive change in that community. It is a public benefit given in exchange for a service to the public good.

LSW: I like this explanation. Within the sector we don't often hear conversations that emphasize the 'doing of the public good'. We're more likely to hear what we 'can't' do or the lack of funding that we have, or that we can't spend money.

LWR: There's a big misconception about tax exempt status and what it means to be a nonprofit. The sector goes by many names, the nonprofit sector, the not for profit sector, the social sector, the independent sector - but however you refer to it, it's not a 'way of life'. You are *supposed* to make money as a nonprofit! You are a business.

LSW: That flies in the face of so much of the behavior that we see!

LWR: It does. The sector operates in this charity model that's been transformed to a poor charity model. We didn't start that way. Yes, we give back to society and serve the public good, but that also means serving as a well-run and efficient - not broke - business. We are a business that is meant to run and keep running. We have operation costs, return on investment, and societal impact that we need to encourage our communities to understand.

LSW: And fundraising doesn't have to be the end all method of raising money, correct? As a business, your nonprofit can also choose to do a social enterprise, a creative means of making money while serving your constituents. And that's important for board members and potential board members to understand.

Fundraising IS important, but so is earning revenue in different ways. As you've said, as a business you're *supposed* to make money. Tax exempt status is simply a status. I think many in the sector look at it and say, well, we can't hire good people because they cost too much and we're "just a nonprofit."

LWR: Yes, tax exempt status means that any money you make is not going to shareholders like a for-profit business. That money goes back into your mission, the profit goes to your stakeholders - those you're helping - as opposed to the for-profit's shareholders.

LSW: You make me think of Dan Pallotta as well, the author of "Uncharitable: How Restraints on Nonprofits Undermine Their Potential." He talks about getting rid of the sense of lack and honoring ourselves with regard to what we're doing. Paying to hire and keep good people who can help your nonprofit do a better job and have greater impact.

I like this overview. This book is meant for both the fundraiser and employee of the nonprofit and the board member or potential board member.

In what capacity does fundraising help support a nonprofit's work?

LWR: Operational expenses are always a challenge and always in need, however donors don't always like to fund operations. Many prefer to fund programs or specific events. That sometimes can lead a nonprofit to create programs just to get the dollars in, and that can lead to mission creep - when you slowly go away from your mission while pursuing funds.

You have to maintain your vision and mission, and evaluate what your true needs are.

LSW: And you can ask for support for specific programs, as you said, or restricted dollars - those funds designated solely to support those specific programs. But you can also ask for unrestricted dollars to help you with those operational costs - which let's face it, includes the staff you need to execute those programs!

This is a great start, laying the foundation to understanding a nonprofit from the outside in. We also need to have a clear understanding of a board's basic roles and responsibilities. It's not just about sitting on a board and coming to five or six meetings a year. Board membership does come with roles and responsibilities, and Liz will walk us through what those look like as they pertain to fundraising in the next chapter.

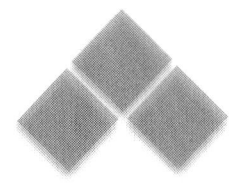

Chapter 2
Basic Board Roles & Responsibilities

LSW: This is an essential chapter for every board member, and the staff training them during the onboarding process. We often miss this step. It can be awkward, even uncomfortable - depending upon your relationship with your board - but it's so incredibly important.

Board members need to know what they are accountable for and why. And both roles and responsibilities are important.

LWR: Yes - and these are based upon the Roles & Responsibilities as outlined by BoardSource, a national organization dedicated to educating nonprofits, consultants and board members about board service. (**BoardSource.org**)

In Roles of a nonprofit board, you're looking at three pieces:

1. Providing adequate financial resources
2. Setting strategic direction
3. Providing oversight

And I like to use the analogy of a three legged stool with these Roles. If you take away any of these three from your board's roles, your stool will fall over. You need all three to be functional.

The very first role, providing adequate financial resources, includes the fundraising piece. It is the board's first role, and includes things like board members making personal monetary contributions, helping the fundraising team bring in new donors, or sponsoring a table at an event. It's not one specific thing, but can be one or several to fulfill the role of providing adequate financial resources.

LSW: Are you looking at each member holding all three of these roles, or are you looking at the board as a whole holding these three roles with individual board members handling each according to their skills? For example, one board member might be better in oversight, another might be better in strategy, etc.

LWR: The board as a whole is responsible for all three of these pieces, and it is the legal duty of each individual board member to make sure these roles are met.

LSW: Legal duty? Tell me about that.

LWR: Yes. There are three legal duties of a board:

1. Duty of Care
2. Duty of Loyalty
3. Duty of Obedience

Duty of Care is specifically related to fundraising. So while the roles themselves may be handled by the board as a whole, the individual board members have legal duties to make sure they are carried out. We'll talk more about that in the next chapter, but yes, it is a legal duty.

LSW: So board members have three main roles, and those should not be confused with the concepts of a working board or a governance board. Those roles apply to all board types, correct?

LWR: Right. And that difference depends upon your board culture. But all three are necessary roles for a healthy and fully functioning nonprofit. I like to say I *serve* on a board versus I *sit* on a board, because those roles do require my active service rather than my passivity.

LSW: Great! I love that. Now take us through the 10 Board Responsibilities.

LWR: I enjoy going through these 10 responsibilities because it always seems to come as a surprise! As a surviving board chair, a surviving board member, I know there is or can be confusion around what a board member is "supposed" to do.

As nonprofits, we need to do a better job overall of educating our board members to these responsibilities, and a great time to do it is during the onboarding process.

The 10 Responsibilities are listed on the next page, but the two that are significant to fundraising are numbers 6 and 10:

- Ensure adequate financial resources, and
- Enhance the organization's public standing.

Basic Responsibilities of GOVERNING Boards

- Determine mission and purpose, and advocate
- Select the CEO
- Support and evaluate the CEO
- Ensure effective planning
- Monitor and strengthen programs/services
- Ensure adequate financial resources
- Protect assets and provide financial oversight
- Build a competent board
- Ensure legal and ethical integrity
- Enhance the organization's public standing

LSW: I'd bet there are a lot of nonprofits who do not know this, but would love to find out! This is interesting.

LWR: It is! And for a nonprofit, fundraising is all encompassing. For example, the 10th responsibility, enhance the organization's public standing, means helping the nonprofit achieve or maintain a good reputation in the community.

Do you have good community relationships? Are you a good community partner? That's where the fundraising comes in. Through this responsibility, the board helps the nonprofit establish adequate community resources, things like in kind services from a printer or accounting team. Different means of saving the nonprofit funds through in-kind services.

It also means bringing in well established persons with philanthropic reputations. And it means ensuring ethical and legal integrity, so potential donors have faith in who you are as a nonprofit.

LSW: I've just had an ah-ha moment. I think many times we look for certain skill sets from potential donors, skills they can bring to us like accounting or legal skills, in the hopes that they will use those skills pro bono as board members.

But, it's also about what roles they play in the community. If you're looking to enhance your nonprofit's reputation and you have a board member who is from a well respected firm, they will enhance or improve your reputation by association and serving on your board.

LWR: And when you start to think about your reputation and what you need, that's starting to think about your board culture which we will talk about that in a chapter later in the book. But it's also thinking about which board members or potential board members are dedicated to your mission and connected in your community. Once they know and understand the roles and responsibilities of a board member, they can help you in the overall fundraising goal.

LSW: Excellent. These points are also skirting the discussion of the ethical and legal basis to board roles and responsibilities, so join us in the next chapter and we'll take a look at why board members need to fundraise.

Chapter 3

Why Do Board Members Need to Fundraise?

LSW: We've just looked at the board's roles and responsibilities, both as a whole board and as individual board members. Now we're taking a look at the legal and ethical duties. What does it mean for a board to be 'required' to fundraise?

LWR: You know, the number one thing I hear is that nonprofits don't know how to motivate or coach their boards to fundraise. And this can be a scary thing. You don't want to take a brand new board member and throw them to the wolves.

LSW: But there is a responsibility for the board to fundraise. So what do you recommend a nonprofit can do when, like you've mentioned, they're not sure how to motivate or coach the board member?

LWR: I always recommend starting by educating them. There are three legal duties as we mentioned in the last chapter:

1. Duty of Care
2. Duty of Loyalty
3. Duty of Obedience

These are required of every board member during board service. The Duty of Loyalty and Duty of Obedience really speak to potential conflicts of interest of board members serving on multiple boards, and which nonprofit they are fundraising for in their particular efforts.

The Duty of Care speaks directly to fundraising, helping the nonprofit raise funds, or finding in-kind contributions. Every board member has a duty to care for the nonprofit they are serving. Now, that looks differently for different organizations and different board members, skills sets, and so on. But it's important to know that this is a legal duty.

LSW: And because it's a legal duty it's vital that every board member knows about it! So tell us now about the ethical duties.

LWR: Any entity serving the public good is in the public spotlight, and any entity accepting donor contributions has an ethical responsibility to those donors to spend those contributions in the manner in which they were intended.

Transparency is also a large part of serving the public good, so all records should be available - with the exception being the privacy of the donors' personal or gift information if they've requested anonymity.

The ethical piece also means being 'above the fold' - making sure your entity doesn't get into the paper for anything other than good news.

Also, ethics includes *the perception of ethics*, meaning, if you're organization is not as transparent as it could be, the public court may hand down an opinion regarding your actions that is less than favorable, and could even break trust with your community.

LSW: And one of the board's biggest responsibilities is the public standing of your organization, so it's essential that your board members are educated about how you're spending your money, why you're making certain decisions, all of that.

Sometimes we think fundraising is just about the money coming in, but it's also the knowledge of how that money is spent and the decisions behind it.

LWR: Exactly, that's donor stewardship. And I want to talk about the transparency of board giving. I believe every board member should make a meaningful gift to the organization they're serving. A meaningful gift may be different from one board member to another based upon their current life situations.

I also believe that if you're thinking about serving on a board, but you are not in the position to make a gift of any kind, you should reconsider. Serve on a committee instead.

LSW: Every nonprofit would love to have 100% board giving! What are some other ways board members can also contribute?

LWR: BoardSource has a great list I've included in this chapter. Everything but doing the 'ask' - asking a donor for

Individual Board Member Participation in Fundraising

- Make meaningful contribution
- Identify, evaluate, and cultivate prospects
- Make introductions
- Organize and attend special events
- Attend face-to-face solicitations
- Write or sign appeal letters
- Thank donors

The Board's Role in Fundraising

- Ensure development plan and monitor progress.
- Create fundraising and donor recognition policies.
- Ensure fundraising methods adhere to ethical standards.
- Participate in fundraising.
- Monitor progress and evaluate outcomes.

BOARDSOURCE
© 2013 BoardSource

money, to cultivating prospects and even making introductions for the nonprofit to community members.

Organizing and attending special events is a popular way for board members to fundraise and "friend-raise".

LSW: Friend-raise, I love it! There are a lot of ways to look at this, and what you're saying is, in addition to all board members contributing monetarily, they also have ways to contribute to your fundraising efforts throughout the year.

And your donors want to know this too, how much skin does your board have in the game? Not just the percentage of your board who give monetarily, but how else do they help you fulfill your fundraising goals, in order to fulfill your mission?

LWR: Fundraising looks different for every organization depending upon your culture or size of your nonprofit. When you're asking your donors to give, but you yourself as a board member have not given, your "ask" has a lot less weight. By giving, you're saying you truly believe in the organization you're serving.

LSW: Before we go on, I want to thank those of our readers who are serving as board members or have in the past. You are making a huge difference in your community through your service!

It's important for us to recognize and remember the commitments our board members have made and are making, including the length of time of their service. Which leads me into the next chapter, and understanding that relationships do take time.

Chapter 4
Building Relationships Takes Time
(Or, Fundraising is a Process)

LSW: Building relationships *does* take time. Those of our readers in fundraising and development really know this. It's not a snap your fingers and get a million dollar gift routine, it's not about whether or not you're "passionate enough" or a good salesperson about your nonprofit. It's not buying a car! It IS more of a dating process.

So let's talk about this from two points of view, the first being to educate our board members about the process, and also from the standpoint of what the board member's expectation should be for themselves about how long it might take in building a donor relationship.

LWR: Taking the first point of view, sometimes our board members do expect new CEO's or Executive Directors to come in and immediately turn things around. If the CEO/ED is a CFRE (Certified Fund Raising Executive), then they have a better overall view, more knowledge about development perhaps, than one without.

So hiring a CFRE for those positions IS a great place to start, but it's only a start. When it comes to being new to the organization, that person is probably not going to have the relationships to immediately ask for money. They will need to work on building those relationships. But, the people who do, or who should, have relationships with current donors, are the board members.

What I often see a board do is invite a seasoned fundraising executive into their organization and expect them to turn around the funding situation within an unreasonably short period of time. To successfully do that requires a partnership between the board and CEO/ED.

I want to emphasize the point that donor relationships should not be with one person, your fundraising person. They need to be with the board as well because our boards are actually in place longer than most of our staff! The transition becomes easier.

LSW: You make me think of Jerry Panas, author of 19 books about the fundraising ask. He's a proponent of that partnership, with a board member and staff member going to donor meetings together. It makes a lot of sense.

And the relationship helps make the board and your leader or fundraising person more of a team, so it's not us and them.

LWR: Absolutely, and it's important that board members are part of your fundraising team as well. Fundraising is not a stand-alone process. It's relationship building, both externally and internally.

LSW: Excellent. Now let's address the second part of my question - is there a relationship building timeline? Can you say from A, the point at which you meet someone to B, the point at which they give a gift, how long that should take? I know we sometimes have this perception that "a good fundraiser" can "close the deal" in X amount of days or weeks. Can you speak to that?

LWR: Of course. The reality is yes, you want to have a goal and maybe even an outline of a timeline in mind, but you also have to understand that everyone's ability to give is different and you have to understand your donor's life and other demands might impact their ability to give.

Have they had a life-changing event? Are the kids going off to college? Accidents? Illnesses? New homes? People don't meet you and instantly throw everything out there on the table. Trust takes time, confidence takes time.

LSW: Exactly. Like we said previously, it's like a dating game. Imagine going on a blind date and the person you've just met says they want to run off and marry you.

Now sometimes that might be romantic and could become the top movie of the year! But most often, it's creepy, and you want to run away.

I like the subtitle of this lecture that you've also said it's a process, a relationship building process.

LWR: We as nonprofits do this when recruiting board members too. All too often we approach someone about serving on our board, a very serious commitment, when we barely know them, they've barely had a chance to get to know us, and that's not the right time. We have to develop those relationships as well, see if we have comparable values.

Or, we approach a first time donor about being a board member, and that's also acting in reverse. We need to find out about the fit before launching into a desperate clingy situation that scares off someone who may become an even bigger, more passionate donor - and who knows, future board member!

LSW: And I'll bet some of our readers may have had that experience and may have a bad taste about serving on a board. So relationship building works with donors, board members, even potential staff.

Great discussion, Liz. Thank you. Now we're moving into our next section, leaving the basics behind and venturing into your current climate.

YOUR BOARD'S CURRENT INVOLVEMENT IN FUNDRAISING

Chapter 5
What Is Your Board Culture?

LSW: Starting off this section, we're looking at where your board currently is involved in your overall fundraising. To get there, you need to understand your board culture. Liz, what is that?

LWR: Board culture is sometimes seen as this nebulous piece, but it really is your organizational values and systems within that make up the dynamic of your board. Look at it this way: If someone walked into your board meeting, what would it look like to them? I'm talking about how they would perceive your board, your nonprofit's relationship with them, your internal values, the overall feeling of how your board relates to each other, your staff and how they relate to fundraising.

LSW: I'm glad you said "nebulous". How do you get a tangible feel for that?

LWR: One model to find out your board culture is to see where you are. There's a phrase, "Be where your feet are." Stand in your space and assess by talking to your board members and your staff. Have conversations about how your staff, board and donors feel you are presenting your values to them, and to your community.

Your newest board members can offer you a lot of insight because they've just come in and formed a fresh opinion.

You can also utilize qualitative and quantitative pieces you can find online for board self-assessments, or have consultants come in and walk you through that process.

LSW: Do you think you can also gauge the atmosphere, such as whether you work and play together well, plan together well, discuss new ideas and initiatives well, or is it the flip side that your board has difficulty even discussing one idea and following through let alone a change?

LWR: Absolutely. I have a friend who says, "Culture eats strategy for breakfast." (laughing) If your culture is politely dysfunctional - or not so politely dysfunctional - you chance having strategy go awry, and that includes fundraising.

So I advise you to start where you are, look at your values, the dynamics of your board, what is the board and staff relationship look like, the peer-to-peer interaction on your board look like, and how the board feels about serving on your board.

We talk a lot about time, talent and treasure needed on your board, but at the end of the day, this is a volunteer service. Do they have warm fuzzies or are they counting the days to get off the board?

LSW: Just simply having those conversations with your board will give you a lot of information, and you might find that their past behavior doesn't reflect your expectations. In other words, there may be some miscommunication going on.

I worked with a nonprofit a few years ago who really wanted to increase their board's overall giving percentage. They wanted 100% of their 30 board members to give - monetarily - to the organization. Unfortunately, they had something like 10 people, maybe 30% giving.

So the CEO began having conversations, and wouldn't you know it, most of them were *not even aware that it was expected* and once they found out they wrote a check on the spot! Here the CEO was thinking the board was slacking, but in reality, they didn't know it was expected! So those conversations will also reveal for you things you may think to be true, to actually be false. In a positive way you could find out your board culture is healthier than you think!

LWR: Right, clear up the confusion if there is any. And also get a gauge as to how they feel about serving on your board. I've had the opportunity to serve on a number of boards and I've walked in as a new board member to several and felt tension, anxiety - not a very good feeling.

If it feels combative, negative, emotionally abusive, you need to know that. It's not a one-time conversation, it should be a regular assessment or conversation between the CEO/ED and individual board members.

LSW: And I want to stress that if you do have a dysfunctional board, if you're serving on a dysfunctional board, turn to someone like Liz who is a Certified Governance Trainer to do the "fixing".

It's always helpful to have someone from the outside coming in, a third party to work with you rather than the CEO/ED trying to get the board to shape up and potentially injuring relationships even further.

If on the other hand, you find you have a fairly good culture or your culture is where you thought it would be and you want to begin working the expectations toward fundraising, how do you do that?

LWR: A couple of things: If fundraising is already part of your culture, it makes it a lot easier to express those expectations. If it's not, look at where your feet are. Do you have conversations with your board members about fundraising? Have you? What did they look like? If you haven't talked with them at all, what does your onboarding process look like? How can you change it or add in the fundraising aspect?

Start slowly and be easy on yourself. One of my mantras is that the best part of board service is that the board is made of people, and the hardest part of board service is that the board is made of people.

Everyone's an individual, and honor that individuality but know that you can empower them in a meaningful way. They are on your board for a reason, find out what it is if you don't already know.

And, what do they want to get out of their board service?

LSW: Love it! And that leads us to a nice segue into the next chapter, which is the Give or Get Policy.

Chapter 6
The Give or Get Policy

LWR: Having a Give or Get Policy is a great way to ensure your board's engagement in the fundraising process. You're asking your board members to either give a certain amount, or get a certain amount - that is bring dollars in - to your nonprofit organization.

When it comes to fundraising, the "get" is not necessarily money, it could be in-kind services or sponsorships. And the give or get is offered as an 'either / or'.

LSW: Either, or. So the board member is not required to do both, correct? You're asking them if they're able to give money as a gift, but if not, or if they can't make a large gift, they can subsidize if you will, by bringing money into the organization?

LWR: You have to start with your board culture so you know what that culture currently is. If you're board is currently NOT fundraising, the give or get policy could definitely be an either/or - as in, this year please give five hundred dollars or get five hundred dollars brought in.

But, if your culture currently includes fundraising in some capacity, this policy can expand upon what your board is already doing. You have to look at it from where you are.

Personally, I think it's important for smaller boards or boards not actively giving 100% that you institute the give OR the get to generate at least 100% activity if not 100% giving.

LSW: Sure, I'm thinking of the fundraising events when you have corporate sponsors who buy a table or two, and those sponsorships might be five, ten or even fifteen thousand dollars. So the 'get' is great if your board member 'gets' his or her company, or another company to become a corporate sponsor.

LWR: Yes, and it empowers the board member while also bringing in another community connection - that corporate sponsor now has your nonprofit on their radar. It also inspires other board members to get their company to become a sponsor or provide an in-kind service.

LSW: And that can become a healthy and fun competition among the board.

I like the way the give or get policy takes the pressure off the board and doesn't make the board member who might be a young professional feel "less than." It gives everyone a way to contribute to their ability.

LWR: Yes. The Give or Get Policy could be vague - especially if you don't have a current policy in place. Or, you could be very specific and say your Give or Get Policy is to give or get one thousand dollars per year, and that allows flexibility.

For example, a board I served on allowed us to combine the two, so if we could not give one thousand dollars, we could give one hundred, then get another nine hundred in sponsorships or in-kind services.

Others may say, we expect you to give or get for a specific event. It depends upon your culture, your budget, and your organization.

LSW: Say I'm a nonprofit newly encouraging and setting expectations with my board members. What would be reasonable to start with?

LWR: That conversation starts at the board level. Your board needs to talk amongst themselves with your CEO/

ED and honestly talk about how you measure fundraising success as a whole, and how willing your board is to newly commit to the expectation.

Often, in these new cases, boards will really jump on it and have fun making it a friendly competition. And keep in mind, you may also lose board members. Some may not be able to fulfill the expectation or don't like the expectation.

That also means those board members who are staying are educated and empowering others as they come onto the board to step up to the plate, so to speak. And that creates a stronger fundraising board.

LSW: Oh, and wouldn't every nonprofit love to have a strong, fundraising board that's engaged and empowered! But to get there you first have to know your board current comfort level with fundraising, which we'll discuss in the next chapter.

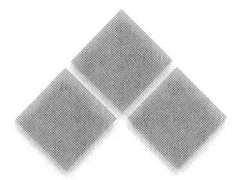

Chapter 7
Assessing Your Board's Comfort Level with Fundraising

LSW: This could be really interesting if you never had the conversation with your board about getting them actively engaged in fundraising. So how do you go about assessing their comfort level?

LWR: BoardSource has a wonderful list of 40 things they can do to fundraise, and I've highlighted a few of my favorites in the graphic on the next page. But what I like to prompt board members with is a little challenge to find one thing they think they are currently good at doing and one thing they could take on as a learning activity. That's enough to ease them into the process without being very uncomfortable.

Individual Board Member Participation in Fundraising

- Make meaningful contribution
- Identify, evaluate, and cultivate prospects
- Make introductions
- Organize and attend special events
- Attend face-to-face solicitations
- Write or sign appeal letters
- Thank donors

It gets the conversation going. And you can simply ask them, in groups or individually, how do you feel as a group about fundraising, and then one-on-one how they feel.

Ask what they've done in fundraising if they've served on other boards, or what was successful, or what they might want to learn to do.

LSW: Yes, because you can have a spectrum of board members - on one end those who sweat and break out in hives at the thought of fundraising, and on the other those who love to ask and get involved in raising money for your organization.

LWR: And you know many CEO's or ED's might think they'd love to have ten of those board members who love to ask, but I'd caution against that. The Ask is just one piece of the fundraising process. You need the relationship builders and those who love to thank the donor.

But the reality is, not everyone is comfortable asking so find something that they like to do.

LSW: Nor do you want someone who is uncomfortable with the Ask, doing the Ask! In Fundraising Success: The Complete Development Plan, Sara Leonard speaks to this. Don't put those folks in charge of the Ask if they're not good at it!

LWR: There's a lot of opportunity with your board members about where their comfort level is. And we need to honor that.

Professional fundraisers understand that they will probably get a lot of no's, but some folks really don't like it. But, those board members could also help with giving tours of your facility, or speaking to their Rotary chapter about your nonprofit, or any numbers of things that fit their skill sets and talents.

LSW: So would you also include those other aspects of fundraising when you're having the conversation about their comfort level?

LWR: Absolutely, because you don't want your board members to run away if they think fundraising is only the Ask. It's not, that just one phase of the process, as we've said. But once they can become engaged in something they like to do, magic happens!

LSW: So step one is to gauge their comfort levels, then the next step is to assess their readiness, which we're going to talk about in the next chapter.

Chapter 8
Assessing Your Board's Readiness to Fundraise

LSW: Once you've had conversations with your board members about their individual comfort levels with fundraising, it's time to gauge their readiness. They can be comfortable without being ready, and it's the work of the nonprofit to get them ready! So how do you know when someone is truly ready?

LWR: It's tied directly to your fundraising goals, your fundraising plan and whether you have one. If you do have a plan, you probably have a priority of attainable goals before you, and that's where you will start in connecting your ready board members to those goals.

If you don't have a plan, it's an opportunity to start from scratch and think about how you'd want to get your board members involved with the activities you already do. For example, if you do tours, you may include your board members in those tours, maybe even ask them to host a tour.

LSW: You're setting measurable goals.

LWR: Yes. That's one part of being ready, setting those measurable goals. The next part is deciding who's the best fit (not just most comfortable) but the best fit for the activity of that goal. A new board member may be comfortable with the fundraising, but is not 'ready' to lead a tour of your facility. So they can help in thanking donors until they've built their knowledge of your nonprofit and can move into the role of tour leader.

Fundraising is not only a relationship process, it's also a team responsibility. It doesn't fall to just one person, but to everyone. Seeing how everyone can play their roles as best fits their comfort levels and readiness is very important.

LSW: Those individual conversations you've had with each board member will help you better determine both comfort level and readiness. Anything else?

LWR: Yes, there are several online board self-assessment tools that may come in handy. And the information you get from these self-assessments gives you a great deal of data on your board readiness and skill sets. In fact, BoardSource has a few at www.BoardSource.org.

And keep in mind, even if someone feels comfortable at the beginning of an activity, that can sometimes change as they learn more of what the activity includes. So readiness is vital to knowing where you are, who can handle (and wants to handle) what, and how you can approach your goals.

You can empower your board members as well with partnering them by their readiness levels, to help them grow into being increasingly ready.

LSW: That makes me thing of two other pieces in this Fundraising Success series, The Complete Development Plan and Creating an Annual Marketing and Communications Plan. Both of these address in different capacities, how your board can play a role in marketing/communications, or in assisting your development team, and how important it is to know *what they want to do* in their board service!

LWR: Yes, and that's why we started with knowing your board culture. That defines your organization's fulfillment of your fundraising goals.

What does fundraising mean within the parameters of your board culture? That should align with your development plan and your marketing and communications plan.

Just be careful of the temptation to over-analyze which leads to "paralysis by analysis". Be prepared to know that whatever you've planned is also organic and will probably change!

And you need to be aware of your board members lifestyles.

LSW: Yes, knowing you have an accountant on your board means you would not engage that board member in heavy activities at tax time!

LWR: Probably not the best time to get them engaged, but then they could be auditors and that time is not as heavy for them as for others. You have to know your board members lifestyles.

LSW: This section has really been about taking a good look at who your board members are, what your relationships with them look like, how comfortable they are with fundraising, and how ready they are based upon your development plan or current fundraising activities. Now we move into the next section which is about getting your board ready through motivation strategies and other educational techniques designed to prepare them better.

Getting Your Board Ready

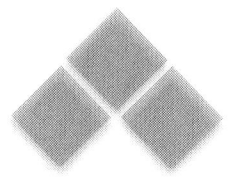

Chapter 9
Motivation Strategies

LSW: Once you know your board culture, the comfort level of your board members and if they're ready, it's your job to connect them with the right activities and motivate them. Before we launch into this discussion though, it's important to address some of the misconceptions many nonprofit staff and board members may have about the nonprofit sector that can greatly affect your board's (and staff's) eagerness to fundraise!

LWR: So, so true. The chief misconception I've seen is how so many folks in this sector hold fundraising as a negative activity, like it's panhandling.

We're seeing a shift in our culture about empowering donors, and helping them use their dollars to make positive change in our communities. We're almost flipping it on its head as the generations shift. Millennials really get this. They see how important and empowering it is to be able to use your money to impact your society in a great way.

LSW: So first, if your organization has any thread of this perception in its culture, pull that thread.

LWR: Yes. And we're also seeing the move from acting as a charity to actually being a nonprofit, and that means recognizing ourselves as businesses. We are here to make money and that's what our donors should expect. It really is about empowering our society to fulfill a mission.

To give to a nonprofit, is giving that donor the opportunity to make change. It's empowering. And when the donor can see what a significant difference they're making in their own community, we're helping them achieve personal satisfaction.

LSW: We all want to know our lives have meaning, and so we need to see it as helping our donors identify that for themselves by giving to our nonprofit, rather than begging them for a handout. I love this!

And corporations are really getting this now, too. There is even a new corporate designation called the B Corp which is given to corporations focused on societal change. They still are a for-profit but want to give back to the community. I think of Tom's Shoes, and how they have a policy of giving one pair of shoes to children in need for every pair they sell. Its social business or social corporations.

So when you're talking about this philosophy, you're talking about a philosophy that corporations already get - and chances are your board members work for corporations like that!

LWR: We have a tendency in our society to look at what's going wrong, but this model flips that on its head. We need to look at what's going right. That's motivating. That's impactful. That's fulfilling.

We're a business. We're meeting a societal need, so it's not begging or panhandling, it's creating societal change, and won't you join us?

And yes, corporations get this. It's not an "us vs. them" piece. We're all part of the community.

LSW: Right, so your board members work their day jobs understanding and wanting to make societal change. When they step into their volunteer role, we need to help them see they are now fulfilling their desire to make personal impact.

LWR: That falls to us in the nonprofit sector. We need to educate the community in a positive manner about what we do and why it's important, starting with our board members.

LSW: And that leads us so well into our next chapter in which we're really going to look at some ways to educate and co-educate our board.

Chapter 10
Board Member Education

LSW: Liz has confessed that this is her favorite subject, board member education, which makes sense as you are a Board Governance Trainer!

LWR: Yes, and also a former school teacher! (laughing)

LSW: So what does this look like? Are we talking about consultants, or classes, or board mentoring?

LWR: Yes! To all, and more! The reason I get excited about board member education is not just because I'm a surviving board member and I've survived board chairmanship. It's also because I believe education comes from various levels. My grandmother said before she passed, "The truly educated never graduate."

When it comes to board culture and learning about fundraising, we always have something more to learn.

There are so many ways to educate your board, whether it's utilizing a portion of your board meeting as a dedicated five minute educational period, or through a board portal on your website, or bringing in a consultant or instructor.

But the most impactful is, I believe, peer to peer education. As a consultant, I can come in and walk your board through levels of learning. But at the end of the day, I'm leaving. Your board is there for each other through their terms, hopefully; and creating an environment where they are comfortable learning from each other is the best way to continue consistent board education.

LSW: And your board members can relate to each other's experiences in ways only your board members understand!

LWR: Yes. Having the opportunity to share experiences and stories also helps them in a way that's truly relevant to your board.

I've also included a list of some of my favorite board education resources at the end of this chapter. And I'd recommend turning within your community to your community foundations and/or what are called MSO's, (management support organizations) which in many geographic locations are the educational hubs for nonprofits.

LSW: If you simply google "Nonprofit Center" or "Nonprofit Studies" in your area chances are good you will find a MSO within 100 miles of your location.

LWR: And 99% of the time these MSO's and Community Foundations do have training or know of some training for board education and governance.

LSW: True. And I'm with you, in my experience it's the peer to peer education that is the most effective, especially if it's in terms of matching the more experienced board members to the newer board members in a mentoring capacity.

LWR: We also should add that there are a lot of great books, a lot of great online resources. And one of my favorite books is titled, "Not on This Board You Don't". It's a playful, easily digestible look at board governance, fundraising, and a board's responsibilities.

LSW: It doesn't have to be dry, like Robert's Rules of Order! I'd also recommend diving further into this curriculum. This book is a summary transcription of the full 3+ hours of video online course, and you can find more information on that in Appendix B of this book, and check into the rest of the Fundraising Success series.

Another method of education is readily available within your nonprofit, and that's the development team, which we'll discuss further in the next chapter.

Chapter 11
Working with Others in Development

LSW: One of the best partnerships within your nonprofit can be between your development people and your board members. So let's talk about what that might look like.

LWR: For the best working relationships, your board should have an understanding of the staff roles of both your development people and your CEO/ED. Sometimes the lines can be muddied, so it's essential to understand the relationships and set the communication lines from the start. You don't want your board members running to your development team and by-passing your CEO/ED, unless of course your CEO/ED is also your Chief Development Officer. You have to know what the internal politics are for your organization and be clear with your board about what that looks like.

The best development people want to engage the board in the process. They want to bring them along on an ask, get them involved in a tour, find out who the board members know in the community or among their donors to help strengthen those relationships further.

A skilled development professional knows you can't just throw out a net. You have to spear fish, if you will. So I'm not saying get the board member to reach out to his or her contacts haphazardly, there should be a strategy used and discussed by the board member and the development person.

LSW: And you're not talking about a board member taking on the staff role responsibilities.

LWR: No, ma'am. I'm talking about having open dialogue about what fits. It means having the board member introduce the development person, be there to help establish rapport and a relationship with the development person. The board member is opening access to their network, getting the development person in front of someone to then begin to cultivate them as a donor.

LSW: What's reasonable to ask of your development person? It may be the board member approaching the CEO/ED to say, "I'd like to get more involved in the fundraising process, can I tag along?"

LWR: First, let's look at the board's expectations of development people and let me cover a few points.

1. What worked in another organization may not work in this one. I've sometimes seen board members come from having served on other board, and in joining the new board they bring expectations set from other organizations. Each nonprofit is unique, and it's important for board members to understand that.

2. What may have been standard practice for another development professional, may not be standard practice for this one. That includes development people from other nonprofits and even development professionals in the same nonprofit. It's important to really look at the individual staff members strengths and how they match the nonprofit's needs.

LSW: Good points. It ties into both the staff understanding their board members strengths and the board understanding their staff/development team's strengths.

And, sometimes we have the reverse, as I mentioned. A board member wants to get more involved, so what is appropriate? Can a board member become a CFRE? Should they?

LWR: They *can* become a CFRE, but should they is the question. You may have development professionals already on your board and they could well be CFRE's. There are a number of qualifications before going through that certification process. But it goes back to your culture and you want to be sure that if a board member does go through the certification process, that they are still following well defined paths regarding the board role versus the staff role.

LSW: And even if you don't necessarily go through the certification process, there are fabulous resources online to help guide you further in working with your development team. There are a number of great articles on the Association of Fundraising Professionals website, which is an international organization.

LWR: Being involved on the local level with your AFP Chapter offers a number of benefits including networking with the top development people in your area. So for example, as a board member, being involved with AFP could help you find a new CEO/ED or Chief Development Officer if you need to begin a search.

LSW: So there are a number of ways board members can work more closely with the development team and learn more skills if they choose. And, as we'll see in the next chapter, sometimes the best method is to act it out.

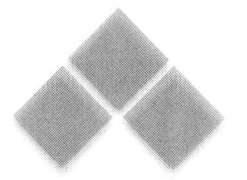

Chapter 12
Role Play in the Board Room

LSW: As we continue to discuss ways to get your board ready to fundraise, we're turning to one method that you can offer to your board to allow them to practice in a safe space.

LWR: One easy way to role play is through developing what is often called an elevator speech. You want it to sound conversational, not over prepared or rehearsed, and yet it also needs to speak to your mission and in a personal way to the board member's passion around your mission.

There's a great quote by Carol Weisman that says, "How many of you have ever raised money in an elevator?" No one!

Your elevator speech is your connection to the mission, what your mission is, and what your 'ask' is - that is, what you want people to get out of your personal involvement in your mission.

I recommend board members pairing up to both craft and practice their elevator speech. They will take turns role playing as a donor and board member. You can even have a team of three with someone playing donor, another playing board member and the third person being the CEO/ED or CDO.

The point is it's an opportunity to practice and think through your personal connections to the mission, and it's an opportunity to practice your interactions with a donor, asking them questions and answering their questions about the nonprofit you're serving.

LSW: And I like that this is done in a safe space. Yes, for some folks it might be a bit uncomfortable to start, but in a safe space you'll quickly adapt and get used to it. It even becomes fun between colleagues and really gives you the chance to learn how you talk about your organization.

LWR: You can also add in a fourth person to act as observer, who can then give you impartial feedback, and the four of you can rotate among those roles.

I do recommend that you take time to debrief after a *real* conversation with a donor as well! So this can become part of the culture of your board, to get feedback and really learn from and with each other.

LSW: You might have some board members who don't want to role play, and that's ok too. But this is a great tool to help your board members find out how they speak about you. Of course, you're not going to force them, but if a few of them do role play and then can speak to the value in it, it could become a regular tool you use.

And, as Liz said in another chapter, share those experiences! That's incredibly valuable.

Chapter 13
Building Your Development Plan with the Board

LSW: The concluding chapter in this section on getting your board ready is a deeper dive into building your development plan *with the board*! For those readers who have not read the first book in this series, Fundraising Success: The Complete Development Plan, let's talk about what a development plan is.

LWR: A development plan is like a strategic plan on steroids. Your strategic plan is about your strategy, how it relates to your mission - most of the time that's going to include development.

Your development plan is the activity you're doing to get there. It is an opportunity to engage and empower the board. And I don't know how you can develop a good, robust development plan without including your board!

For example, one piece of your development plan may include major gift giving. Your board gives input into defining how big that gift is - is it five thousand? Ten thousand? Your board also gives input into whether your organization is ready to pursue major gifts, and whether you know any members of the community you want to cultivate to become a major gift donor.

LSW: It really does pull your board members into your organization. I like the emphasis on engaging and empowering them. They are part of your team.

LWR: We talked about legal duties and requirements of board members - those are really the bare minimum required of their board service. And getting them engaged in the creation of your development plan from the start is essential. They must be informed about the fundamentals aspects of their role and that includes understanding where they play a part in conceiving and executing your development plan.

LSW: So if you do already have a development plan in place but it doesn't necessarily include your board, now's the time to educate them! Work it into your next board meeting and share with them what your organization is doing to fundraise.

LWR: And find time to explain to them and educate them about how and where they fit in.

LSW: For more information on the actual creation of a development plan, read Fundraising Success: The Complete Development Plan, or take the expanded online course, which is also approved for 3.5 CFRE credits. You can access the course through this link:
www.bit.ly/FS1BOOK10.

Ways Board Members Can Assist in Fundraising

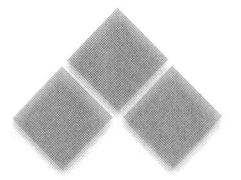

Chapter 14
Ways Your Board Can Participate in Fundraising

LSW: This section is the actionable, how you can task the board with certain activities to help with fundraising. Not everyone has the same skill set, nor do they have the same interests. So what are some goals we can set for our board members, or activities to drive them to action?

LWR: We've talked about several of them and I'll refer again to the BoardSource checklist for board members. It's a wonderful tool and lists dozens of ideas and ways in which board members can get involved. A lot of them are about working with staff from the ground up, that is, creating the development plan and guiding the organization with definitions of where you are now - what does a major gift mean to you? What's a reasonable goal for an event?

And then you get into the next phase of cultivation - what donors should we focus on cultivating and growing?

LSW: And who can we introduce to the organization. I'm thinking of board members and their networks.

LWR: Yes, who can we introduce since some of your board members might be very connected within the community. Also, who can we invite to tours? Or taking a deeper look at some current donors to explore their passions further and find out what it is they want to accomplish with their giving.

Then you have the solicitation, the Ask. And the other piece where board members can participate, and frankly my favorite, is stewardship.

It is so wonderful to spread gratitude in a world that doesn't always have as much gratitude as we'd like. Stewardship is a great way board members can be involved and assist in fundraising.

LSW: And who doesn't like to pick up the phone and say, "Thank you for your gift"?! It's a great feeling to be able to thank someone and they in turn feel good too.

LWR: Absolutely, and when you make that call, leave it at that. Don't ask again, just genuinely thank them!

LSW: This makes me think of the Give or Get Policy and how you can divvy up responsibilities among your board members.

Now, once your board members have their designated tasks, how do you hold them accountable to them?

LWR: Very gently! This is where the peer to peer interaction comes in. We talked previously about building a fundraising culture within your board, and part of that culture includes accountability. If you have fundraising goals, how are you as goals holding each other accountable?

You can do that a number of ways. You can designate a certain portion of the board meeting to following up on activities, you can have certain ramifications or cause and effects for things that don't get done - again, gently.

You need to have a designated name to the activity. If a board member has been tasked with an activity, put their name down. The more action oriented you make it, and tie it to a specific person, the less likely you will have the committee say, "Oh, I didn't know I was supposed to do that, I thought it was such and so."

Be specific. If Robert agrees to invite three people to next month's tour, write that down and give him a deadline to give the names to your staff.

LSW: And in the board meeting, have a tour report so Robert knows a summary of that activity will be available for the board to review, whether in a dashboard or in a committee report, and he's more likely to get it done.

LWR: Your meeting minutes are a great opportunity to report back to the board as a whole. Did the activity happen? If not, why not? How can we help? What do you need from us as the board or us as the staff? It's your comprehensive action plan for your team, free of judgement but also an accountability plan.

I want to stress that this should be empowering, not judgmental. It should uplift your board members, not beat them down. We want to celebrate their successes and find out what the challenges are so we can help, or we can all learn from that challenge.

LSW: I'm hearing you say that accountability looks like setting the activity, stating the person who's accountable for that activity, targeting a due date, and reporting back to the board as a team. That makes sense, and everyone's on the same page.

LWR: And following up in between meetings too, you don't have to wait. Sometimes it's very helpful to your busy board members if you can find out ahead of time where they are and serve as a gentle reminder to get the info to you or act on their activity a few weeks before the board meeting. People respond really well with that kind of leadership, and you're setting them up for success.

Chapter 15
Board's Role in the Ask

LSW: We've talked through the past few chapters about how your board members - or you if you are a board member - have different skills, talents, and desires in helping with your fundraising activities. What if your board member want to become involved in the Ask? What should you say? Is it ok?

Some nonprofits don't want the board doing the Ask if they are not a trained development person, and yet, the board member may be very eager to help! We turn to our expert Board Governance Trainer, Liz.

LWR: First we need to ask if the eager and enthusiastic board member is capable of making the Ask. Yes, they may be excited and poised to connect with their networks and make the Ask.

This is where having a development professional on your staff is extremely helpful, even vital. The development person can sit down with the board member and walk them through what that looks like. Invite them to observe you making an Ask, or several different scenarios.

LSW: Ok, yes. So while the board member may be eager and enthusiastic, they may also have no or little development training. They might miss subtle opportunities that an experienced development person would be alerted to toward developing that relationship further.

LWR: Yes. It's like modeling or cross training. If you've ever been to a restaurant and a waiter is in training, and the experienced waiter says, "This is John, he's shadowing me today in training."

Similarly, your development person can say to your donor, "This is John, one of our amazing board members, and he wants to learn more about our organization and ways he can communicate with his network. He's not going to be asking anything today but is preparing to participate in a bigger way with our mission. So he's listening to what you and I talk about today, and please give us your honest feedback during our conversation."

LSW: That's great! Not only does it make the donor comfortable immediately in spite of having an additional person present, but it also give you the opportunity to hear real feedback from your donor.

LWR: Sometimes our board members just want to know what the ask looks like, what do you say. But the bigger reality is that the Ask is about framing the conversation.

As Carol Weisman so astutely says, when we're talking with donors it's not about our story, it's about their story. How is their helping us, helping them?

Another aspect to that is that our interaction is about making a human connection. It's not just about asking for money. It's about connecting our donors with our mission, showing them they are making a thoughtful impact.

LSW: I really, really like that. Sometimes we can get caught up in seeing the donor as a piece in our fundraising jigsaw puzzle, and you're saying, pause, take a real human minute to connect. That's essential for the board members to understand as well.

LWR: Yes. And while you're there, it's another side to relationship building. With your board member present, it gives you the opportunity for real feedback from your donor, not just about the current conversation, but if you have the time, stretch it out. What are we doing well? What would you like to see us do differently? Your donors are a great source of information and will be exceptionally honored to be asked, and asked in front of a board member.

LSW: I like this for multiple reasons. It gives the board member the opportunity to learn. It gives you the chance to reflect on your fundraising tactics and skills. And you can use it all the time, not just for an educational opportunity! You can invite board members to come with you for this purpose anytime.

It also eliminates the "I think" zone. That's when you come back to your development meeting and someone (or you) says, "Well, I think they're not ready," or "I think it might be too soon."

If you're saying "I think" then you *don't know*. And this scenario of donor feedback can remove that temptation to jump into the "I think" zone.

LWR: I've seen it work really well between a board member and CEO/ED or CDO. And you sometimes see this shift happen. The board member may start silent, but towards the end of the conversation, they are making the Ask.

LSW: And it's a comfortable learning environment!

LWR: For everyone.

LSW: Yes, for everyone. I love that. So our next question follows, what is the board's role in stewardship? Join us in the next chapter.

Chapter 16
Board's Role in Donor Stewardship

LSW: We've talked a little bit about this, and how it can be a great way to get your board involved in fundraising.

LWR: When it comes to donor stewardship, we need to start by asking how we, as a nonprofit, are thanking our donors. How are we recognizing them? It's part art, part science.

If you have a donor database, even if it's just an Excel spreadsheet, you have some history, some data to be able to track a history of giving. The more robust your database, the more ability you have to run reports on your successes, on your donor's giving history.

So once you've looked at your donors and you know their history and track record, or you know they've come into an inheritance or something else, you also know how you've recognized them.

Do they have a name plate? Is there name on the building? Have they been in any philanthropic news articles? The art of stewardship then is about taking all of this information to be able to weave it into a meaningful conversation with your donor.

LSW: Ah, yes. So your board member needs to know how to do that as well. How to continue to enhance the relationships you already have. Donor stewardship is not "just" about writing a thank you note!

But you bring up an interesting point which leads me to a couple of questions. First, how much do you want your board member to do in helping you gather the kind of data or information you'll record in your database?

Secondly, would you ever open your database up to your board member?

LWR: Let me start with the second question first. Absolutely not, for several reasons. First, you can have too many people inside of your database and that can generate chaos and a poor data collection method. Second, your donors may not want other people outside of the designated development people in your organization to know their personal information, their addresses, their contribution history, and on and on.

LSW: Yes, I know as a former financial advisor, there are legal ramifications regarding people's personal information or gift amounts. That includes even your staff, so you need to know who should and shouldn't have access.

LWR: Your database holds very confidential information, and only the select staff should have access. That said you do want to be able to let your board members know as it's appropriate, who makes a gift, or as allowable, what the donor's history is.

LSW: For example, perhaps you have pledge categories of bronze, silver and gold, and this particular donor like to wear his annual gold pin designating him as a gold pledge donor.

LWR: Philanthropy is a very personal enterprise, and you want to make sure you know what the donor wants. That's primary. It's not necessary or even good business to have all staff members have all unlimited access to your donor database.

But, you do need a system in place in order to cull a list of all the people who've given ten thousand dollars in the past five years so you can target them for your capital campaign.

I have also seen situations when there are too many people in your database and it gets confusing and difficult to maintain.

A short answer is this: the day to day access, entering data, culling reports, is a staff duty. If your board wants access, explain the ethical and fiduciary responsibilities you have to your donors. It's a vital education.

LSW: Excellent, thank you. And now a quick answer to my first question regarding what type of information should they be giving back to you to enter into your database?

LWR: Keep it basic, but have a system in place so your board members can report back or bring your development team up to speed on the meeting. Things like children's accomplishments, family happenings both good and bad, anything that will help you in knowing your donor is good information.

You don't need the fine details of what they ordered for lunch, or even where they went - unless the board member thinks the "where" was important. For instance, if they were both at a conference and you want to make note of that. But keep is simple and informative.

LSW: Excellent. Thank you.

Ways Board Members Can Lead Fundraising

Chapter 17
Support and Selection of Your CEO/ED or Chief Development Officer

LSW: This section may catch your attention as it's about how board members can actually *lead* the nonprofit in fundraising. This chapter in particular speaks to that.

LWR: One of the chief responsibilities of the board identified by BoardSource used to be termed, "to hire and fire" the CEO/ED. That's been changed now to "support and select" the CEO/ED or CDO. While "selection" may be fairly obvious, to "support" looks differently among different nonprofits.

Basically, support refers to a partnership. It's information coming from the board about prospective donors, grants, etc and information from the staff about the successes of programs, fundraising and so on. It's a two way street.

Support for a CEO/ED or CDO refers to a board's understanding that the CEO/ED/CDO position is very difficult and respecting what that entails. On the flip side it's the CEO/ED/CDO knowing they cannot successful run a nonprofit fundraising effort without the aid of the board. It's the board who are connected to the community and potential donors.

LSW: In an earlier chapter we talked about the board understanding what to expect of a new CEO/ED/CDO. This goes hand-in-hand with that. And it's expanding upon that.

How many nonprofit CEO/ED's have confidence that their board members truly understand their jobs, know their staffs - and I don't mean personally, but have a professional understanding of the responsibilities of the staff - and can speak competently about those roles?

LWR: It's also knowing that there is a board manual as well describing the board members roles and responsibilities.

Knowing that the average shelf life of a development professional is about eight months in an organization is motivation enough for board members to have a fuller understanding of what they do. The turnover rate within the nonprofit sector, while sad, is fact - it's very, very high. If a donor is thinking about a major gift, is eight months enough time to build a relationship to get that gift?

If the gift comes in, it's usually because there was a longer relationship in place with a board member.

LSW: So that speaks to how essential it is for board members to have an intellectual investment into their nonprofit as well. They need to be knowledgeable about donor relationships, as we've said before, because the development professional may not be with that nonprofit as long as the board member is. And if the development professional is the only one with the relationship, then that donor relationship may follow the staff member to his or her next position.

LWR: Yes, and it's the CEO/ED/CDO's responsibility to support the board also. The CEO/ED needs to be tasking either themselves or their lead development person with educating the board on prospects, successes, major gift relationships, etc. If that person is a CFRE, they can do a little coaching of select board members interested in participating in 'Ask' type conversations with donors. But it is a staff responsibility to keep that communication and education line open.

LSW: And that's empowering to both the staff member and the board member.

LWR: Let me speak to one more aspect of that. Yes, it's empowering, but it's also the opportunity for the board member to find a more personal connection with the nonprofit mission.

Perhaps the board member does not yet have his or her own "mission moment". The development professional can introduce the board member to a client or donor who carries a passion for your mission, and let the board member and the client or donor connect. The goal is for the board member to be able to relate personally to your nonprofit's impact. That goes hand-in-hand with keeping those communication and education lines open, and assists the board member in fulfilling the "support" end of the 'support and selection' we're talking about in this chapter.

LSW: I love it! Let's do talk a little about the selection term, even though it seems obvious.

LWR: Sure. You know, the purple unicorn of selection of the CEO/ED is to find someone who is amazing at accounting, who is a phenomenal fundraiser, an inspirational leader and manager, and on and on.

LSW: Pie in the sky dreaming, right? Doesn't every nonprofit board want that? But it's so very rare - the purple unicorn!

LWR: Right. And we've just talked about the average development professional shelf life being eight months. CEO/ED burnout is also very real and can be a threat to your nonprofit.

I encourage the board to do more listening in the CEO/ED selection process than asking. Yes, ask the basic questions pertinent to your organization, but also listen to the questions your CEO/ED candidates are asking.

If you're looking for someone proficient in development, that candidate should be asking about your fundraising goals. If you're looking for a partner to work with your board and the nonprofit staff, they should be asking partnership questions such as what is your culture? What is your stewardship strategy? What are your fundraising goals and how are they executed?

LSW: Great points. And we can take that even a little bit farther. Knowing the turn-over rate for nonprofits, is the board selecting someone who can build the bench? Is that person capable of holding a vision further out - five, ten, twenty years, to build the next generations of leaders for your organization? Is there a succession plan in place? Wouldn't that also fall to the board under this "support and select" responsibility?

LWR: Yes, it absolutely would. Succession planning is extremely important. Not just the staff but also the succession planning for the board. The board should be looking at their incoming officers, potential new board members, and so on. You always want to plan for succession if you can.

Even if you have a CEO/ED or CDO that is beloved by the community, you need a succession plan in place for when that person leaves.

LSW: That ties directly into your fundraising plan because you have to have a transition and you have to have a leader. Without the leader, your fundraising plan may come to a halt, lose momentum, and even begin to crumble.

That's a lot to think about!

Chapter 18
Fundraising Committee
(How to Staff and Support a Committee)

LSW: In this section, we're talking about ways your board members can actually *lead* your fundraising, and the fundraising committee plays a big role in that.

LWR: Committees are where the majority of the work gets done. The board level is about high level, generative, governance decisions. The committee is where the board, staff and community members focus on the steps needed to achieve those decisions.

Committees serve as fabulous recruitment grounds for potential board members. It's an opportunity for them to get to know you as an organization and for you to see what they can bring to the table, a way to vet each other if you will.

The fundraising committee is a very important piece of that. The Give or Get Policy could come from the fundraising committee as well as the governance committee. The structure depends upon what your organization's need is.

The fundraising committee is a great way to bring people in to help you with the fundraising process without being at the leadership level of your board. That said you do want at least a couple of board members to serve on your fundraising committee.

LSW: So how do you go about asking your board members to be on the committee? Should there be a policy in place stating board members are required to serve on a committee?

LWR: Start with your bylaws. Your bylaws are documents that you create which then state 'by law' how your organization will operate.

LSW: And to emphasize what you've just said, they are not laws in place somewhere on the state level. These are rules you've created for your nonprofit, and according to the state you must operate by those standards that you've created.

LWR: And they can be amended if needed. I'd recommend taking a look at your bylaws annually and seeing how do your by laws say your board members are participating? Do your committees require a board member to chair them?

The fundraising committee may require the entire board to serve on the committee or a certain percentage of the board to serve on the committee.

LSW: The committee lets you get a top down and bottom up view of the fundraising goals and activities you've planned. And to your point, it's a fabulous recruitment ground for potential board members.

So maybe your bylaws say in order to become a board member you first need to serve on a committee for two years. That gives your community member the opportunity to really get to know your nonprofit before board service.

The other aspect to serving on the fundraising committee that I really like, is for those board members who want to become officers of the board. In order to become Treasurer, they should definitely have participated on the fundraising committee prior to holding that office.

LWR: Yes, and it ties directly into board roles and responsibilities. It's ensuring you have adequate resources but it's also providing oversight. It does not mean you are implementing the nitty gritty of the fundraising plan, that's a staff function.

LSW: Yes, and being on the fundraising committee is one piece of the fundraising team - the team being a much bigger body which includes the committee, and you can learn more about who should be on your fundraising/development team in Fundraising Success: The Complete Development Plan.

Another aspect of board leadership is through serving as a donor, a sponsor, or both. We'll explore that in the next chapter.

Chapter 19
Serving as a Donor/Sponsor

LSW: As we discovered, there are a number of way our board members can lead our nonprofit in fundraising. Sometimes we think it's about how we can lead them, but there are several key areas they lead us. Liz, why is the donor/sponsor role important?

LWR: Let's start with why it's important for 100% of our board member to give. If a board member is approaching a potential donor/community member and asking for a financial contribution, it's much more impactful and has more weight for that board member to be able to say, "Will you join me?"

The Ask is about joining the board member in making a contribution, in joining the board member at their table for the event. It's collegiality. Many board members are peers with your donors.

When they can say philanthropically and peer-to-peer that your nonprofit is important to them, they can also speak philanthropically to the potential donor.

LSW: They're leading by example.

LWR: Yes, and making the connection. Showing potential donors how good it feels to give to your organization and why.

LSW: So what would be appropriate for a board member to give to be a donor or sponsor?

LWR: That flows with your nonprofit and/or the fundraising event. If it's a gold tournament, the board member could sponsor the hole-in-one event. If it's a luncheon, sponsor a table. If it's an online give day, how is the board member encouraging online gifts in that 24 hour cycle? Are they motivating their friends on social media?

It depends upon what your current fundraising activities are and your overall development plan.

LSW: So this is an opportunity for the CEO/ED to see what those activities are and how to encourage the board to participate in them.

LWR: Yes, that's where you really want to get board members engaged so they begin to think about how they can create a friendly competition amongst themselves. It becomes fun a peer to peer interaction, think of new, out of the box ideas to bring in new donors or new gifts.

LSW: You've just made me think of a win / win / win. If you have a board member who is a sponsor for an event, you have the opportunity to recognize them by putting their logo on your brochure, table plate, etc. It's a win - they're an engaged board member, win - they're sponsoring your event, win - they receive recognition in the community for serving as a sponsor and the rest of the community at your event sees their philanthropic expression.

It's doesn't have to be huge!

LWR: And I think it's absolutely important that your board members are contributing financially. Sometimes nonprofits invite major donors onto their boards without holding them accountable to further giving. So my caution is about bringing donors on, because they then become legally responsible to your organization in that position.

If they don't want to be legally liable or accountable for oversight, invite them to serve on an advisory council instead.

LSW: And you are about to segue right into the next chapter, when we talk about board members leading with challenge and matching gifts.

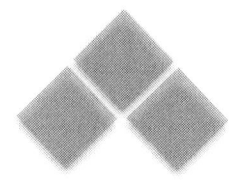

Chapter 20
Challenge and Matching Gifts

LSW: Let's start this chapter by talking about the difference between challenge gifts and matching gifts.

LWR: A challenge gift is when a board member (in this case since we're talking about board engagement) will put out a challenge to the community or fellow board members. It may look like a "meet or exceed" such as — "I'm giving $5000 to this organization and I'm challenging you, the community or the board, to also give $5000."

Sometimes, a person responding to the challenge may also work for a company that will match whatever that person gives. Say I work for Corporation A, and in response to the $5000 challenge I do my part by giving $1000. Then I can apply through my employee portal with Corporation A and my company will then hand in another $1000 toward the challenge. The Corporation's gift is considered to be a match, and together with my corporation I've been able to contribute $2000 toward the $5000 challenge.

Challenge and match gifts can really do a lot to motivate support. And the challenge piece is saying, "I've put my money where my mouth is, join me."

LSW: So in that example, does that mean the $5000 challenge is not paid if the match is not reached?

LWR: It depends on how they define the challenge. Sometimes it's simply that, a challenge. Other times, it may come with a caveat, "We'll pay $5000 IF you match it." The goal then being $10,000.

Or sometimes the challenge issued will match UP TO a certain amount. I would caution against the IF scenario because you could be setting yourself up for failure. Instead, consider the UP TO scenario, then you will always receive a certain amount of money regardless.

LSW: It's meant to inspire friendly competition and excitement about the fundraising activity.

You see that in the online give days, when certain corporations will offer prize pools for certain times, like whichever nonprofit brings in the most gifts between 1 and 2 am, the ABC Corporation will give a $2000 prize. Your board could then also throw out a matching gift UP TO the $2000 prize money if your organization wins that time block. You're generating excitement and encouraging more people to give because they see that their gift will bring even more money into your organization.

What are some creative ways board members could push out challenge and match gifts?

LWR: One really successful way I've seen is for board members to push out VIP tickets to some sporting event. Or tickets to meet someone, say a speaker, backstage. Those types of tickets generate immediate excitement and often your board may even buy them up!

I've also seen board members "reward themselves" by planning for an award ceremony at the end of the fiscal year. The reward is to recognize the board member who brings in the most corporate sponsorships, or new donors, or whatever the competitive goal is. And the reward could be a plaque, but for more excitement it could be tickets to a sporting event or something that excites your board.

LSW: It's really about putting that FUN in fundraising! I love it. These are some very creative ways your board can lead your fundraising efforts.

Now we're moving into another very important section, which is about how to evaluate your board's fundraising.

Evaluation of Your Board's Fundraising

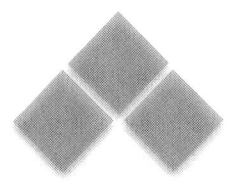

Chapter 21
Sharing Successes at the Board Level

LSW: Let's start by asking why it's important to share successes?

LWR: We talked about fundraising being a learning experience. So it's important to start the experience by focusing on the high point so that we have the energy and willingness to look at the challenges.

LSW: That makes sense and it's motivational. People who feel disappointed or unenthusiastic about something don't necessarily want to learn anything else, we naturally become disinterested.

So, when is it appropriate to share successes? And by that I mean specifically about a major gift, perhaps a donor you've been working with for a while finally makes that major gift. When is it appropriate to tell the board? Who do you share it with first? Is there political etiquette involved?

LWR: It's about the culture of your board, your nonprofit, and your donor's preference. Here are a few examples:

If it's something that you've been expecting for some time and your board is aware of the possibility, and your donor is well known to several of your board members, it's probably a good idea to let your board know immediately. Why? Because then they have the opportunity to reach out to their colleague and thank them personally, and that may feel really good for the donor.

That said, you may have donors who wish to remain anonymous but are still well known by some board members. You have to respect the donor's wish to remain anonymous, it's NOT OK to tell them, even 'confidentially' who that anonymous donor is. Yes, you can share that you received the $50,000 gift, but not who it is.

It's about being respectful of people and their wishes.

LSW: Great point, and sometimes it's not a whopper of a gift but sharing the smaller successes is important as well.

LWR: Yes, like the little tangibles that come with an event: tickets sold, attendees registered. All of those are important to the board, both from a financial oversight position as well as personal motivation.

You can also share tangible successes from tours of your facility, how many people come through, how many new donors come in through tours, and so on.

LSW: Yes. When you have those tangible things that creates encouragement!

LWR: Absolutely, and social media and online fundraising can really create that, so be sure to post, tweet and share your successes in fundraising and friend-raising.

LSW: I love the friend-raising! There's also the flip side of this coin, how to share challenges at the board and committee level. And as we'll see in the next chapter, it doesn't have to be a bad thing.

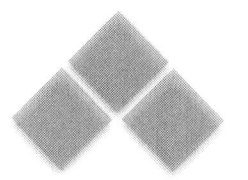

Chapter 22
Sharing Challenges at the Board and Committee Level

LSW: Sharing successes is always fun. Sharing challenges can be...challenging! So why is it important?

LWR: It boils down to history. If you don't want to repeat the negative aspects of history, you need to share challenges. It helps to organically determine the framework of an issue moving forward.

I personally love the Nelson Mandela quote, "I never lose. I either win or learn." This can speak to building a culture of fundraising resiliency. It's not an acceptance of failure.

Instead, it's an understanding that not every Ask will be a yes. Not every "No" will be a never. As a fundraiser, you have the ability to build that resiliency. Nobody likes hearing "No", but over time, you come to an acceptance of it and even an appreciation for it, in order to grow, in order to learn.

LSW: What a great way to see that!

LWR: And from the board level, in a non-confrontational yet strategic way, it's important to review what you did and why it didn't work. Did you ask too much? Not enough? You don't know unless you ask.

LSW: And you don't know what has and hasn't worked in similar instances unless you talk, unless you share. Your other board members or staff are your number one resource for information and experience.

How can you present it to your committee or board without it seeming like a failure?

LWR: I recommend getting into the habit of always debriefing. What worked, what didn't, what can we do differently? Each time you have that conversation, it becomes more and more part of your natural routine.

I always say start at the micro level, meaning, start with those involved first, discuss what worked, what didn't and what you can do differently among yourselves. Then take it bigger: to the committee level, then to the board level.

LSW: I see what you're saying, so by the time you're at the macro level, the board level, you're not talking in terms of the actual conversation but a bigger picture that fits into your overall fundraising methodology.

That takes away the human inclination to turn it into a blame game and shoulder one person with everything that's wrong in the world. There's a lot more going on than perhaps one person's fundraising skills. If you address it as a blame game, you don't build your organizational skill sets.

LWR: Yes. With an Ask it's easy to celebrate and move on, and in the nonprofit sector we rarely take time to pause and reflect, whether as an individual, team or larger group. But we need to. We need to create a culture of acceptance on our boards, cultures that uplift, that offer opportunities of mentoring when needed.

LSW: I'm thinking of specifics, when you might have one board member who consistently makes poor choices, not intentionally of course, but just due to lack of experience or knowledge, and so on. If that person were a staff member, their supervisor could bring them aside and coach them. But how do you handle it when it's a board member?

LWR: Gently. First of all, I never believe in calling people out in front of the entire board. That creates a defensive atmosphere which is the exact opposite of a learning atmosphere. Instead, have an individual conversation with that person - and since it's a board member, that would best come from the board chair.

LSW: What if it IS the board chair?! (laughing) You know that's happened sometimes.

LWR: (Laughing) Sometimes it is the CEO or ED who has a conversation with the board chair, but typically it's a tough conversation that should be handled by someone else, for example the Chair elect. The CEO/ED can't necessarily ask the boss why they dropped the ball! But perhaps they can talk with another board member who can have a one off conversation with the board chair.

The bottom line is that the goal is to create a culture of openness and accountability, and know as a group what you are holding each other accountable to and for. You can't allow one weak link to continue on the board and sometimes that means you might have to fire a volunteer. That's not easy either, but if the culture itself is in place, it's navigable, and you're less likely to have drama around that particular issue.

Remember, your nonprofit is a business. The board is accountable for making sure your business is meeting your mission, and if you have a weak link that's preventing you from meeting your mission or achieving your goals, you're responsible for addressing that.

LSW: Communication is the name of the game. You have to have an environment that allow for all forms of communication.

Chapter 23
Celebrating and Acknowledging Good Board Behavior

LSW: It's incredibly important that we celebrate our victories, our successes and our board. So when is it appropriate to acknowledge a board member or your board as a whole?

LWR: I would say it's usually always a good idea, but there can be more significant celebrations. If you've had one board member finish a task that was important to your fundraising objectives, and another board member brought in a multi-million dollar gift, they're both important but should not be celebrated in the same way. If you do, you risk altering the value of each.

LSW: I see. You could celebrate one verbally and one in an email for example.

LWR: Yes. You could acknowledge the task accomplishment in your board meeting with a thank you, and you could acknowledge the multi-million dollar gift in your e-newsletter or an email to your board and staff.

But think of the ways you can celebrate the good: in your social media, in your e-newsletter, in your quarterly report, in letters to your donors, in your board meetings.

If you know your board members well, you'll also know who they look up to or admire. You can ask a board member whom they admire to call them and say, "Great job!" Having someone we respect validate what we've done is a great way to receive an acknowledgement.

LSW: And there are ways the board as a whole or a committee achieve something great. For instance, the search committee may be looking for the next CEO/ED and after an eight month search, they've found an excellent candidate. How can you celebrate the success of that committee's achievement?

LWR: Of course you can celebrate them at the board level, but there's also an opportunity with achievements like that for self-assessments.

It's a great idea for your board to do a self-assessment annually.

LSW: Awesome! What does that look like?

LWR: There are a number of board self-assessments available on line, for instance from BoardSource. Self-assessments can help you answer things like:

What went well this year and what role did I play in that? What challenged our board this year and what did I learn from it?

The board can then share those answer with each other and truly learn from those assessments, while taking the time to appreciate the work they've each done, acknowledge that work and celebrate what went well.

LSW: Great exercise! Is this something you can do at the committee level as well?

LWR: Absolutely. That's a really important level to have evaluation and assessments because that's where a lot of the board work is actually being done.

And the committee level is also a great level to have social sharing, meeting socially to celebrate like after an event is completed. It's important to add some fun into the work to keep your volunteers interested in coming back and staying engaged, whether as board members or community volunteers.

LSW: That's a big one. How often do we see board members serving for two, three, five years, but never fully recognized until their leaving? Then they receive a plaque and a hand-shake "thank you" and we move on to the next board member.

What your saying is incredibly important. Board members are volunteers. They're working with us toward a goal, but they're not salaried employees. This is vital to the health of our board.

LWR: Celebrating your board is vital at all levels, and as you think about the different successes they have, find ways that match the success to honor them.

LSW: Very important. Thank you for this very important section on evaluating the board's fundraising.

Now we'll move into a section you titled, "Other Thoughts" which starts off with a bang, the subject of how to recruit fundraising board members, which we all want to know!

Other Thoughts

Chapter 24
Recruiting Fundraising Board Members

LSW: One of the biggest questions we face in building our boards with members who are dedicated to fundraising, is exactly that - how do we find fundraising board members?!

LWR: This is where I sometimes say tongue in cheek, just pray. (Laughing) But truly, it's not about finding people who are seasoned in fundraising, it's also about finding people who want to build a skill set.

When you're recruiting board members, you also want to find out what they hope to get out of their board service. Find out if they want to build a fundraising skill set.

Maybe they want to build their networking abilities or add a development skill set to add to their own resumes.

LSW: What kind of questions can you ask in that recruitment process? Can you ask if they know how to fundraise?

LWR: Absolutely. Your questions are also laying a clear foundation that if you serve on our board, you must fundraise or participate in fundraising. And you need to know what that means to your organization.

LSW: Right, what does it look like?

LWR: Yes, what is the participation, for example. You may have 100% participation and let them know that. Ask what their experience is in fundraising, what is their skill set in fundraising, what is their comfort level in fundraising?

I also encourage you to ask potential board members, "What do you want your legacy of service on our board to be?" Their answer will give you a good idea of what it is they are looking to accomplish by serving on your board.

You can add to that by showing them how significant it would be if their legacy of service included helping you generate funds, develop a Legacy program, launch a capital campaign, bring in major gifts or establish an endowment fund.

LSW: And you've included a great resource in this chapter about questions to ask when you're recruiting.

LWR: Yes, and I want to caution folks against making it too complex. Be honest, be up front about your expectations, and know that it's a two-way street.

If they feel validated, they will very likely extend their length of service (i.e. term). But in order for you to connect with that you need to find out what they're looking to do. And with regard to the list, pick a few, don't feel like you have to ask them all of them.

LSW: Each individual is different and each legacy of service will be different, so choose accordingly.

I like how you're connecting with the board members even before they're elected onto the board. That's starting a culture of openness and communication immediately, even beginning in the recruitment process.

Board Recruitment: Questions to Consider

- **What is your board culture?**
  - How do you promote trust, information sharing, teamwork and dialogue?
- **What are your needs?**
  - Board Member Matrix/Inventory
  - Interview/application process in place
- **What is the level of commitment expected of board members?**
  - Time, Talent and Treasure
- **What can you offer them?**
  - Why are you unique? How well do you achieve your mission work?
  - Do they have access to other board members and CEO/ED?
- **What do they/you want their legacy of service to be?**
  - How can you help them to ask this question up front?

Chapter 25
Duty of Loyalty & Conflicts of Interest

LSW: Early in this book we briefly touched on the Duty of Loyalty. This is such an important aspect, and involved legal parameters. Liz, what is it?

LWR: The Duty of Loyalty is part of your legal requirement as a board member. It means that if you are sitting on multiple boards, you are legally required to be true to your mission. That becomes fundamentally important with regard to fundraising.

Let me give you an example. I serve on two boards, one is a lemur protection agency, the other is a predator agency. That's obviously a direct conflict, so the question is, where is my loyalty in fundraising? Am I fundraising to keep the species alive or feed the predator?

LSW: Yikes!

LWR: You might have a similar comparison if you serve on the board of an agency fighting a certain disease, and on another board of an agency involved in the interests of a pharmaceutical company. There may or may not be a direct link, but you need to ask where your loyalties lie. If they are split, you have a conflict and cannot be loyal to both.

LSW: Can that also apply to individuals serving on too many boards? That you cannot possibly have the time or capacity to be loyal to all of them?

LWR: Absolutely. I know a lot of our community members may choose to "sit" on a number of boards. But 'service' on a board is where I'm encouraging people. You want to make sure you're following and fulfilling your roles and responsibilities for each and every board.

How much energy do you have to support the boards you serve? Are you fulfilling your roles and responsibilities?

LSW: To that point, I know within our own community there are certain individuals who are so sought after to serve on boards that they may have to say no or step away from service if they are honestly wanting to fulfill the roles and responsibilities. That doesn't mean they are not passionate about your organization, they just don't have the time.

LWR: I met someone recently who frankly stated that she serves on a number of committees but only serves on two boards. That way, she can be involved with the nonprofits she cares for, but she's only financially and legally responsible to the two boards she's serving. So that's a great way to be more involved if you want to be while upholding the Duty of Loyalty...get involved at the committee level.

LSW: Excellent. And as you showed at the beginning of this chapter, serving on multiple boards can create a conflict of interest. You and I have previously also discussed how someone who is a fundraising staff member of one nonprofit may be asked to sit on the board of another nonprofit in the hopes that that individual with fundraise for the second nonprofit - that too, is a conflict of interest.

LWR: Yes. And when it comes to conflicts of interest, there needs to be a policy in place at the organizational level and your staff and board are disclosing at least annually, their potential conflicts of interest.

It's part of your organization's Form 990 and required for all staff and board members participating in your organization.

If you do not have a list of each of your board members potential conflicts of interest, you need to do that. They need to list each agency they are involved with on a board level that may pose a conflict for their service with your agency.

If you were to search "conflict of interest nonprofit" you will pull up a lot of examples. Or, I'd recommend reaching out to your local MSO (management service organization) for help in creating a conflict of interest policy.

The conflict of interest is part of the Duty of Loyalty and not a choice, so it should be explained and signed in the on boarding process of the board member.

LSW: Thank you for this. We're moving now into our summary and resources section for a quick review and guide to the resources included in this book.

Summary and Resources

Chapter 26
Conclusion

LSW: Congratulations! You've worked your way through Fundraising Success: Board Engagement and Empowerment in the Fundraising Process, with an incredible amount of valuable information put together by Liz Wooten Reschke, co-author of this book.

Thank you, Liz. It's been a comprehensive conversation.

LWR: And my pleasure! I hope our readers have found it to be valuable and a great resource to continue to turn to for questions. We've covered quite a bit here:

We started by looking at the importance of fundraising in the nonprofit sector as a whole and understanding where your board is in relation to that. We looked at determining their comfort level and getting them ready to fundraise. We saw both how your board members can assist and lead in the fundraising process and when those are appropriate.

We wrapped it up by learning how to evaluate and celebrate your board's fundraising efforts, and I think there's an opportunity for both of those. And we ended with looking at the legal duties of board members, and how you can begin to intentionally recruit fundraising board members.

LSW: Liz also put together a variety of resource materials you've seen throughout the individual chapters. We've included them all in Appendix A.

This is meant to be a living, breathing, organic process you can use year after year, so keep Appendix A nearby to use as your continual resource guide as your board's grow and change.

This book is a summary transcription of our fuller online course, Fundraising Succe$$: Board Engagement and Empowerment in the Fundraising Process, which is approved for 3.5 CFRE Points.

Use this link to get the course at a 10% discount: **http://bit.ly/FS3BOOK10.**

Thank you, and good luck with your plan!

APPENDIX A

The following pages contain the resource documents and templates used throughout this book.

Basic Responsibilities of GOVERNING Boards

- Determine mission and purpose, and advocate
- Select the CEO
- Support and evaluate the CEO
- Ensure effective planning
- Monitor and strengthen programs/services
- Ensure adequate financial resources
- Protect assets and provide financial oversight
- Build a competent board
- Ensure legal and ethical integrity
- Enhance the organization's public standing

Board Education Resources

* Connectivity Community Consulting (ConnectForMore.com)
* BoardSource (boardsource.org)
* Board Builders (smallboardbuilders.com/operations)
* Association of Fundraising Professionals (www.afpnet.org)
* Independent Sector (independentsector.org)
* National Council of Nonprofits (councilofnonprofits.org)
* Your Local Management Support Organization – For example, Nonprofit Leadership Center of Tampa Bay (nonprofitleadershipcenter.com)
* Nonprofit Consultants Connection (nccfl.org)

Board Members' Legal Obligations

- Duty of Care
  - Using your best judgment
  - Actively participating, paying attention
  - Asking pertinent questions
- Duty of Loyalty
  - Avoiding conflicts of interest
  - Putting aside personal and professional interests
- Duty of Obedience
  - Staying true to the organization's mission
  - Obeying the law, both public and organizational

Board Recruitment: Questions to Consider

- **What is your board culture?**
  - How do you promote trust, information sharing, teamwork and dialogue?
- **What are your needs?**
  - Board Member Matrix/Inventory
  - Interview/application process in place
- **What is the level of commitment expected of board members?**
  - Time, Talent and Treasure
- **What can you offer them?**
  - Why are you unique? How well do you achieve your mission work?
  - Do they have access to other board members and CEO/ED?
- **What do they/you want their legacy of service to be?**
  - How can you help them to ask this question up front?

www.ConnectivityConsultants.com

Connectivity
Community
Consulting

©2015 All Rights Reserved

Building Your Board Culture: Striving for Exceptional

7. **Compliance & Integrity** - What policies and procedures exist to ensure the agency stays ethical and compliant?

8. **Sustaining Resources** - What is our fundraising or development plan? How does it relate to the strategic plan?

9. **Results Oriented** - How do we measure success?

10. **Intentional Board Practices** - Is there a culture of board development? Are there procedures and operations in place to help us work towards exceptional?

11. **Continuous Learning** - Are there board orientation and communication processes in place? Is there board evaluation occurring?

12. **Planned Revitalization** - Are there thoughtful term limits in place? Are there recruiting processes ongoing? Is there succession planning for board chair and other officers?

The Source: Twelve Principles of Governance that Power Exceptional Boards

www.ConnectForMore.com

Building Your Board Culture: Striving for Exceptional

1. **Constructive ED/Board Partnership** - What does the ED/Board relationship look like?
2. **Mission Driven** - How do we communicate, measure and demonstrate our mission work?
3. **Strategic Thinking** - What is our strategic plan? Is it realistic and frequently communicated?
4. **Culture of Inquiry** - What is our agency culture? Are we promoting thoughtful analysis?
5. **Independent Mindedness** - Are there any conflicts of interest? What is our COI policy?
6. **Ethos of Transparency** - Do staff, board and others have access to governing documents?

The Source, Twelve Principles of Governance that Power Exceptional Boards

www.ConnectForMore.com

Connectivity Community Consulting
©2016 All Rights Reserved

Fundraising Committees

- Lead board participation in fundraising
- Work with staff to develop fundraising plan
- Develop board fundraising policies, plans, procedures
- Ensure case is strong and based on organization mission
- Lead board effort in identifying, cultivating, and approaching major donors

Individual Board Member Participation in Fundraising

- Make meaningful contribution
- Identify, evaluate, and cultivate prospects
- Make introductions
- Organize and attend special events
- Attend face-to-face solicitations
- Write or sign appeal letters
- Thank donors

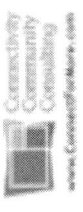

Primary Board Responsibilities

Set Organizational Direction
- Determine mission and purpose
- Ensure effective planning

Ensure the Necessary Resources
- Ensure adequate resources
- Select the chief executive
- Build a competent board
- Enhance the organization's public standing

Provide Oversight
- Monitor and strengthen programs and services
- Protect assets and provide financial oversight
- Ensure legal and ethical integrity
- Support and evaluate the chief executive

Overview: Roles and Responsibilities of...

The Board
- Setting Organizational Direction
- Ensuring Necessary Resources
- Providing Oversight

Individual Board Members
- Duty of care
- Duty of loyalty
- Duty of obedience

- Ambassadors for the Organization
- Volunteers for the Organization

Roles of Nonprofit Boards

1) Set strategic direction
2) Ensure necessary resources
3) Provide oversight

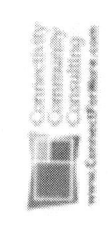

Suggested Readings For Board Fundraising

Fund Raising Realities Every Board Member Must Face - The title says it all.

Asking - Fundraising's ALL-TIME bestseller.

The Ultimate Board Member's Book - Roles and responsibilities skillfully explained.

The Fundraising Habits of Supremely Successful Boards - Cultivate them and double the money you raise.

How Are We Doing? - An end to board drift and procrastination.

Fundraising Mistakes that Bedevil All Boards (and Staff Too) - Wrongheaded thinking exposed.

Big Gifts for Small Groups - For those seeking gifts of $500 to $5000

List from Emerson & Church Publishers (http://emersonandchurch.com/)
Each can be read in 60 minutes

The Board's Role in Fundraising

- Ensure development plan and monitor progress.
- Create fundraising and donor recognition policies.
- Ensure fundraising methods adhere to ethical standards.
- Participate in fundraising.
- Monitor progress and evaluate outcomes.

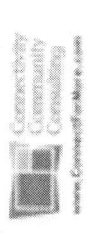

What is your board culture?

How do you promote….

➢ TRUST
➢ INFORMATION SHARING
➢ TEAMWORK
➢ DIALOGUE

List Adapted from Culture of Inquiry: Healthy Debate in the Boardroom by Nancy R. Axelrod. BoardSource, 2007.

Why 100% Board Member Giving?

- Demonstrates personal commitment
- Gives board members confidence to ask others to give
- Encourages other funders to give
- Creates board member "ownership"

Additional Resources:

1. 12 Questions To Ask When Applying For A Fundraising Job (Carol Weisman)

    http://bit.ly/12QuestionsWeisman

2. AFP Article on Give/Get

    http://bit.ly/AFPGIVEGET

3. Change the Way You Look at Fundraising (Network for Good)

    http://bit.ly/changethewayyoulook

4. What Not to Ask When Recruiting Board Members

    http://bit.ly/whatnottoaskwhenrecruiting

APPENDIX B

This book is a summary of the Udemy online course: Fundraising Succe$$: Board Engagement and Empowerment in the Fundraising Process.

The online course is approved for 3.5 CFRE Points and includes:
- 3.0 Hours of HD Video
- Lifetime Access to the Course
- All Resources as downloadable documents
- Further expansion on the topics discussed in this book

To access the course with a 10% discount, and purchase the course with CFRE approval for 3.5 Points, follow this link:

http://bit.ly/FS3BOOK10

About The Authors

Liz Wooten Reschke, MPA, CGT

Over her 20 plus years of service to the nonprofit sector, Liz has served in a variety of capacities including volunteer, fundraising and program staff, board member and consultant for a number of nonprofit agencies in the Tampa Bay and Key West communities, state of Florida, and the United States. Past staff positions include Girl Scouts of West Central Florida, Nonprofit Leadership Center of Tampa Bay, Cystic Fibrosis Foundation and the Florida Holocaust Museum. She has served as a proud member of the Association of Fundraising Professionals, Social Enterprise Alliance, Young Nonprofit Professionals Network, League of Women Voters, Daughters of the American Revolution, and Emerge Tampa. She most recently served as the Founding Board President of Nonprofit Consultants Connection, a membership association of peer consultants that promotes excellence in the field of nonprofit consulting. Liz also served as Board Vice-President for Are You Safe, a nonprofit agency advocating against domestic violence and providing free legal assistance to victims. She is a Life Member of the USF Alumni Association and a BoardSource Certified Governance Trainer.

Liz currently serves as President of Connectivity Community Consulting, Inc. a company that works primarily with nonprofits in the Tampa Bay community. As lead consultant she works collaboratively with her clients to create strategic consulting solutions that address a variety of areas including: nonprofit capacity and community building, organizational development, philanthropic advising, training & workshop facilitation, and coaching & mentoring. She provides trainings on topics such as best practices in board governance, the next generation of nonprofit leadership, and meaningful board service. Her consulting clients include those interested in making meaningful connections in their local communities and the nonprofit sector including: the National School Foundation Association, Gulf Coast Community Foundation and Allegany Franciscan Ministries. Whatever the topic of expertise, Liz's work places focus on community building and resource sharing to help an organization and an individual meet their mission.

Before her career in the nonprofit sector, she worked as an English teacher and dance-team coach in the Florida public school system teaching both high school and middle school in Tampa and Key West. Liz first moved to Tampa Bay to pursue her Bachelor's degree in Secondary English Education at the University of South Florida, where she also earned her Masters in Public Administration and Certificate in Nonprofit Management. These experiences as well as the many educators in her family have instilled a deep belief that continual education is crucial to individual and agency success. Through her current work in the nonprofit sector she develops training courses and curriculum that integrate her love of teaching with her knowledge of nonprofit best practices.

Louanne Saraga Walters

Louanne has coached and mentored students in video production, personal & spiritual growth, social media, organizational management and finance over the past two and half decades, helping them discover, develop and deepen their talents and skill sets.

Louanne has over 30 years in communications, teaching, finance and tourism including:

- A TV news reporter/anchor with three NBC affiliates (KPOM, KRIS, KWQC)
- A video programmer and cruise director with Royal Caribbean Cruise Lines (RCCL)
- A financial advisor with Raymond James & Associates
- Director, Marketing & Communications at the Community Foundation of Tampa Bay
- Instructor to entrepreneurs, small businesses and nonprofits
- Co-Producer and Host of The Philanthropy Show®, an internet talk show program of My Video Voice Productions, the full scale video production company she owns with her wife, Sharon.

Facebook:
LouanneWalters1
MyVideoVoice
ThePhilanthropyShow
The28DayGratitudeWorkout
Twitter: LouanneWalters
LinkedIn: LouanneWalters
Email: Louanne@MyVideoVoice.com

Websites:

MyVideoVoice.com
ThePhilanthropyShow.com
The28DayGratitudeWorkout.com